MW00535329

Tying and Fishing
the
Riffling Hitch

ART LEE

Human Kinetics

Library of Congress Cataloging-in-Publication Data

Lee, Art.
    Tying and fishing the riffling hitch / Art Lee.
       p.   cm.
    Includes index.
    ISBN 0-88011-782-6
    1. Fly fishing--Equipment and supplies.   I. Title.
    SH456.L4   1998
    799.1'24--dc21   97-39318
                                               CIP

ISBN: 0-88011-782-6
Copyright © 1998 by Art Lee

All rights reserved. Except for use in a review, the reproduction or utilization of this work in any form or by any electronic, mechanical, or other means, now known or hereafter invented, including xerography, photocopying, and recording, and in any information storage and retrieval system, is forbidden without the written permission of the publisher.

Cover photograph and all interior photographs by Kris Lee. Interior illustrations by Galen Mercer.

Acquisitions Editor: Martin Barnard; **Developmental Editor:** Kent Reel; **Assistant Editor:** Rebecca Crist; **Editorial Assistant:** Laura Majersky; **Copyeditor:** Jim Gallant; **Indexer:** Prottsman Indexing Services; **Graphic Designer:** Robert Reuther; **Cover Designer:** Jack Davis

Human Kinetics books are available at special discounts for bulk purchase. Special editions or book excerpts can also be created to specification. For details, contact the Special Sales Manager at Human Kinetics.

Printed in Hong Kong   10   9   8   7   6   5   4   3   2   1

Human Kinetics
Web site: http://www.humankinetics.com/

United States: Human Kinetics, P.O. Box 5076, Champaign, IL 61825-5076
1-800-747-4457
e-mail: humank@hkusa.com

Canada: Human Kinetics, Box 24040, Windsor, ON N8Y 4Y9
1-800-465-7301 (in Canada only)
e-mail: humank@hkcanada.com

Europe: Human Kinetics, P.O. Box IW14, Leeds LS16 6TR, United Kingdom
(44) 1132 781708
e-mail: humank@hkeurope.com

Australia: Human Kinetics, 57A Price Avenue, Lower Mitcham, South Australia 5062
(088) 277 1555
e-mail: humank@hkaustralia.com

New Zealand: Human Kinetics, P.O. Box 105-231, Auckland 1
(09) 523 3462
e-mail: humank@hknewz.com

*This book is dedicated to the memory of Glenn Mercer,
gentleman, artist, always a good sport, and to
his beloved Marilyn who hitches our fishing duds
and is sure to make steelheaders of us yet.*

Dear Erin,

Thanks again for your help and support, I look forward to our adventure.

Contents

v

Foreword

When Nat Reed invited three of his western steelhead fishing friends to join him and two other eastern Atlantic salmon experts on the Grand Cascapedia in the early seventies, the results of the informal competition were not surprising. We westerners did just fine and we could see that the other gang would have performed just as well in our own backyard on the west coast. Essentially, the techniques for summer and fall run steelhead are mirror images of those for *salmo salar*; the only differences being adjustments in fly size and speed to compensate for the usually greater aggressiveness of steelhead.

What I remember from that experience that was different from anything we used out west was seeing a small riffle hitch wet salmon fly raise a salmon and although that particular fish was not hooked, it peaked my curiosity and before the week was over I had learned how to make a proper hitch and looked forward to trying it one day on steelhead. Like anything new, however, it takes a while before the right circumstances come along when you have either been doing very well and are so far ahead that you feel you can afford to risk a new, untried technique, or you are so desperate that you are willing to try anything. Before I ever tried the technique on steelhead, I had built up a good deal of confidence using it up on the George River where the vast majority of our salmon were caught using the hitch.

I first started using the technique on steelhead as a means of making dry flies wake more efficiently. We had been using waked dries for some time, but mostly using flies whose intrinsic design was such as to wake naturally. Most of them had the serious defect, however, of riding lower in the surface film with every drift and made it harder to follow and observe the most exciting part, the take. It was years before I started hitching wets. My brother, Pat, tried it fishing with me on the Grande Ronde and caught the only fish of the day and I became convinced. I've used the hitched wet fly often since then. It is often the most effective means of bringing a fish to the surface to take your fly. Very small wet singles are ideal for slow moving water and the larger ones for heavier flows.

This book on the method clears up many of the questions that frequently occur to anyone who tries it. Art Lee's text and Galen Mercer's magnificently clear illustrations remove the mystery from what is, in my humble opinion, far and away the most exciting and satisfying method of fishing for Atlantic salmon and steelhead.

Jack Hemingway, Sun Valley, Idaho

Acknowledgments

I've got a problem. This is my first salmon book—though not my last, I pray—and it's a little book. So how does this essentially city kid with "champagne tastes and a beer pocketbook" who has lived a dream country life, who has, largely by the kindness of others, been granted the opportunity to experience so many of the world's great salmon rivers, thank *all* those who have made that dream life possible? How does he thank all those who have taught him to fish the rivers he has fished, even were he to limit his thanks to those directly involved in mastering the Riffling Hitch? Which wouldn't be fair, anyway, given that "hitch-craft," as my dear friend Orri Vigfússon, angler *extraordinaire* and conservationist *sans pareil*, likes to call it, is, after all, but one course in a sweeping curriculum. In sum, how does he thank them all without making what's called in publishing the "Acknowledgments" section of the book as long or longer than the book itself? Frankly, I've encountered few angling situations so tricky. The agony and the ecstasy is that when so many people, places, and institutions have touched your life, done so much for you, meant and mean so much to you, you can see every face, remember every name. I'm stuck.

So, I suppose my only recourse is first to offer my boundless thanks generically, hoping that at least most of you will know who you are, whether you are still with us or get wind of this book while wading some celestial river teeming with taking salmon. I'm not sure I could find words to thank you properly in any event. Then I'll have to single out a very few, those without whom, absolutely, this book wouldn't be—and I wouldn't be on the horns of this dilemma.

Starting with Mike and Susie Fitzgerald, founders of *Frontiers International,* who have sported Kris and Galen and me all over the globe, never demanding a thing in return beyond honest assessments of what we've experienced. Such generosity and class have always been rare but become even rarer, it seems, year by year, as angling in general, and salmon fishing in particular, become more and more transactional. Had Diogenes' lamp burned just a little bit brighter, I'll wager he would have found the whole *Frontiers* "family" and spent less of his life atub and more of it astream.

Then there are Jack and Leslie Manes who quite literally carried us on their backs through good times and bad. Jack Manes is the most unselfish human being I've ever met. There simply are no words express our gratitude to you both. We will love you always.

Though referred to elsewhere herein, my thanks again to The Atlantic Salmon Federation (ASF) and *The Atlantic Salmon Journal,* to Bill Taylor, ASF president, Philip Lee, most recent *Journal* editor, and Harry Bruce, his predecessor, for all the trouble they've taken to help make this book a reality—and hopefully a success. Thanks, too, to Lucien Roland, ASF chairman (Canada) and to Joseph Cullman III, chairman-emeritus (U.S.). What extraordinary men. A note of gratitude to Dr. Wildred Carter, ASF president-emeritus, who has often been right when I've been wrong and has never lorded it over me. And finally a special expression of thanks to Donal C. O'Brien, Jr., current ASF chairman

(U.S.), for his friendship, loyalty, and sage counsel. Though Don may be the busiest person on the globe, he somehow always finds time for me. Whatever meager progress I may be making in the arena of "people skills" has been inspired in great measure by his example both as a gentleman and a consensus-builder. Neither I nor the salmon—who can not speak for themselves—could have a better friend, ally, and advocate.

We want to thank George "Hadley" Hadley, proprietor of the Cold Spring Camp on Québec's Matapédia River, for giving us a roof, boat, motor, paddle, and pole, plus three glorious pools to fish year after year. Such generosity is almost unimaginable in any age, let alone this one. Likewise, everyone at Árnes on Iceland's Laxá I Adaldal, the most interesting salmon river in the world in my opinion, and the river to which I return every year, not only to catch salmon, but to restore my soul. Völly, Hilmar, Stefan, Petur, Steini (my anchor), and Hemmi—each has helped make us feel like members of Árnes family, and even as I write this, my soul, as well as my mind, count the days until we are all together again.

There is one guy so special that to try to convey his measure literally locks your fingers over the keys. Not because he so graciously agreed to write the Foreword to this book—to speak for me to his fellow steelheaders—but because just to see his smile, hear his laugh, I'd gladly forego a 50-pounder on Alta. Jack Hemingway has long described himself as "the son of a famous father and the father of famous offspring." Frankly, a big part of me wishes neither were the case, for then, clear of shadows, his radiance, intelligence, wit, and talent could be fairly assessed without distortion. A great fly fisherman and wing shot. A thoroughly decent human being. And just for the record, a legitimate war hero.

No book by me on salmon fishing would exist without Richard Nelson Adams, dean of the Matapédia, and perhaps the greatest Atlantic salmon guide in history. Most of what I know of the fundamentals of the sport I have learned from this "force of nature." In a curious way, it may have been one of Richard's countless quips that subliminally, anyway, inspired this book. "It's strange the people who can't tie knots," said 'Himself' to President Jimmy Carter. "Well they tie 'em but i' takes'n ax to untie 'em." Talk about throwing away the mold.

I also want to express my heartfelt thanks to *Human Kinetics*, and specifically to Martin Barnard, the company's acquisitions editor, who saw merit in this little book from the beginning and refused to suffer doubters up, down, or sideways. And to my personal editor, Kent Reel, whom I suspected at first might have been assigned to me purely for pun appeal, until I quickly came to recognize his dedication to making any book he works on the best it can be. In this instance, "Reel" and "Real" could well be interchangeable, for Kent *is* the McCoy.

Thanks to Rudy Romania, Dave Danzig, John Randolph, Ernest and Elaine Alson, Dave O'Brien, Gideon, Riley and Harvey House, Manny Cains and the rest of the Portland Creek gang, Hoagy Carmichael, Alvord Clements, Joan Wulff, Walt and Winnie Dette and Harry and Elsie Darbee, Mary Dette Clark, my dear brother George Scott Lee, Stan Bogdan, Tom Pero, Raymond and Diane Beaupré, Jean-Paul and Peter Dubé, Ásgeir Ingolfsson, Thor Gújónsson, Páll Jónsson, Christian Cyr, Vital Cyr, David Ball, Arsène Dugas, Raymond and Rejéan Pelletier, President Jimmy and Mrs. Rosalynn Carter, Bill Connolly, Ásgeir Haldorsson, Norman and Jackie Lyons, Rod Yerger, The Earl of Kimberley, The Lord Tryon, Gillean Proctor, Nathaniel Pryor Reed, Thorpe McKenzie, Ted Dalenson, David Goodman, Randy

Carlson, Tom Lenz, Stanley Connolly, Dr. Jonathan Sastic and Dr. Gerry Falco.

Inexpressible gratitude to Dr. Ken Stalter for saving my life and to Dr. Kenneth Gordon for making that life better after it was saved.

And finally, to Kris and Galen, my partners, to whom this book belongs at least as much as it does to me. (Hence so many "we's" throughout these Acknowledgments.) Know I recognize that the only difference is that my name happens to be featured on the jacket. Indeed, if each picture is worth a thousand words, then, truth be told, this is actually *more* your book than mine.

INTRODUCTION

I love to fish the Riffling Hitch. So do many of the best salmon fishers I know—including Galen Mercer, my fishing partner, whose affection for the technique, I'd suggest, is reflected in the painstaking care and extraordinary quality of the illustrations he prepared for this book. Ditto, my wife and all-around partner, Kris: nothing will bring her running faster to riverside, festooned with swinging cameras, than a cry that a salmon is "looking" at the hitch and so she might get to record the drama of angler, rod, line, and trailing fish on film. It's just *that exciting*.

But why a little book *entirely devoted* to the hitch—rather than, say, covering the subject within a big book on salmon fishing strategy and technique? And then as a follow-up question, why *this* book, now? The answer to the first question is easy, the latter somewhat more complex and touchy, although I'll take a stab at it.

At different points in the book—the beginning and the end, actually—I express surprise that fewer salmon fishers seem to know how to rig or fish the hitch than I might have expected and that the hitch is a "tool" that I believe for the most practical of reasons, as well as reasons involving pure pleasure, all keen salmon fishers ought to know and use when appropriate. So, you might say it was my aim to see more Vs trailing more flies on more rivers on the one hand, while hoping to guide more anglers into sharing the sheer joy of the hitch-fishing experience on the other.

What I didn't mention in the text, though, was that upon reading countless angling books and magazine articles, I've never felt

I hit upon a single one that fully explicated the mechanics of tying and/or plying the hitch, and frankly, of those that ostensibly sought to, one that made many of the fundamentals, much less the nuances, essential to succeeding with the technique, really clear. I can only hope this one does.

Then, too, I was troubled by evidence that most anglers were convinced the hitch's potential is more limited than my own harvests of anticipation—so many surprises, so many thrills—have proven to me over the years beyond any doubt or need to qualify. My ultimate goal, then, was to encourage not only more anglers to master the technique, but that they use it more often and under a far wider range of conditions than heretofore accepted or recommended. At this, I hope I've also succeeded. The extent to which you take my advice, *and how you make out astream as a consequence*, of course, will, I recognize, decide that.

But, ultimately, I wanted this book to be a "tool," just as the hitch is a "tool." Or put another way, I wanted to make a book that anglers would feel comfortable carrying with them, perhaps even to streamside. A book that didn't weigh you down, nor dictate that you troll protracted indices to find relevant bits you might want or need "on the spot." A flask, so to speak, as opposed to a lead-crystal decanter.

Much of this book began as a series of articles that appeared in *The Atlantic Salmon Journal,* the official publication of The Atlantic Salmon Federation, in 1994 and 1995. That the parts be cast into book form was the brainchild of my good friend Bill Taylor, now the federation's capable president, and Harry Bruce, then editor of "*the Journal,*" as we like to call it, which I'm proud to serve as Editor-at-Large. I'm grateful to both for broaching the idea, just as I was that they found the pieces worthy of publication in the first instance. I also find it instructive, and inspiring, that two men with so much else to do, so much responsibility in the day-to-day struggle to save the world's most politicized of gamefish, were also attentive enough to somehow find time, much less inclination, to spot what could be perceived as nothing more than a single brush stroke on a huge canvas, then go to the trouble to point it out to one person, yours truly, in whom I can only presume they must have had confidence I would make of it something to benefit their larger constituency. Let's hope their vigilance and subsequent faith were well placed.

More research, pleasurable as it was, went into gathering the material for this thing than one might suppose by its weight. That research didn't always lead where I expected or wanted it to end up. From the onset, for instance, I knew I risked taking a lot of spray over the bow when I discovered that what I now am *certain* is the "right way" to rig the hitch on the side of a fly's head contradicted that recommended by one of my personal idols, Lee Wulff. "You're going to hear about this, Arturo, if you put it in print," I told myself with full knowledge aforethought.

And hear I did all right, particularly from some of the "old guard," such as longtime friend Hal Lyman, salmon fisher, conservationist and gentleman, each in full and equal measure. But notwithstanding their position, I thank them for the good will with which they expressed their reservations. Reflecting today, I suppose I should have expected no less from such good sports. Truth is, I wish I had found, and hence had been able to write, that Lee's method was the best, the only method—period. Even more, given I didn't and wasn't, I really wish Lee were still with us, so he could, as I fully recognize he would have, had his say. Since he is not, however, I want the record to show that no disrespect to Lee Wulff was intended. Lee was the greatest salmon fisherman North America has ever produced. He was also a great man.

The rub, so to speak, however, I soon recognized, was actually rooted in that very greatness—Lee's uncanny ability to work magic with rod, reel, line, leader, and fly, to test himself and challenge us until the very end. Fact is, most of us *aren't* Lee Wulff

Angling pioneer Lee Wulff was unquestionably the greatest Atlantic salmon fisherman North America has ever produced. Until his death while flying his own airplane at age 86, Lee challenged us all to push ourselves to the limit by introducing ever-increasing challenges to our angling techniques. It was Lee who popularized the Riffling Hitch which he learned during his years of angling exploration and experimentation in Newfoundland.

and therein lies the definitive criterion. Lee's hitch configuration worked so well for him, yet isn't ideal for most of the rest of us, precisely because *he was so good.*

From the day we begin fishing wet flies for salmon, we are admonished over and over *not to set the hook* when fish take. Hook-setting, I'd guess, costs more salmon than any other blunder. Call it "the itch" or "buck fever"—what you will—how many of us can claim we haven't snatched a fly away from a taker by reflexive hook-setting at that critical instant that so often determines yea or *nay?* Indeed, I lost so many salmon in my early days that my teachers, for purposes of education and damage control, finally demanded I adjust my reel drag to its lightest setting, then place my free hand down the back of my waders. Eventually I learned and can honestly say I haven't made the mistake in years. But, then, I fish salmon 10, 12, and sometimes more, weeks a year, which most anglers don't or can't. And it was to those who don't or can't I felt an obligation when I began putting words to paper while preparing to duck.

I won't go into specifics here, as they're covered further along, except to say that Lee's system more often than not *does* require that you set the hook on hitch-taking fish while mine *doesn't.* Thus, mine, in effect, unifies wet fly technique, at least to some degree, which should prove a certain relief not only to the novice, but also to those who even after an eternity of trying are still too quick to pull the trigger. Perhaps, then, you might choose to call my way, and its dissection here, an exercise in empathy.

While I make at least my quota of errors, on-stream and off-, my top priorities as a writer are, always have been, and always will be, accuracy and clarity. Thus, seeking to recognize my limitations, I endeavor never to address subjects I don't know well. From the outset, therefore, I feel obliged to emphasize that I really know very little about steelhead fishing. Not that I don't admire the species or those steelheaders who have obviously attained, by what I've seen and read, wowsome skills at fishing for them. It's just that being an easterner unabashedly obsessed with Atlantic salmon and on a limited budget—to say the least—I've had minimal opportunity to pursue steelhead and thereby to learn the fine points of that sport. My loss—and one I yearn to rectify.

I have been assured, however, by a sufficient number of experienced and capable steelheaders, including my cherished friend, Jack Hemingway, whose Foreword you've no doubt already read, that this book will be of value to steelheaders, as well as to Atlantic salmon fishers. I hope so. But not, I assure you, simply to boost sales. The chief reason is that since I've learned so much from steelheaders that I now apply to fishing salmon, it would be sweet to think I've returned the favor, if only in small measure.

I suppose I also harbor the hope deep down that this little book will perhaps prompt more westerners to come East and more easterners to go West. To make us more "anadromous," so to speak. For communicating on the "Net" notwithstanding, we still have much to learn from one another, face-to-face and side by side, not only in terms of how to catch those fish that enchant us so, but in terms of working cooperatively to effectuate functional means by which to save these beleaguered creatures of the wild, for our own gratification, sure, but even more to our credit, for the benefit of those still far removed in time from the redds up from which new generations of sportsmen and champions of resource conservation will someday swim.

"RIFFLING" RIGHT

ince Lee Wulff brought it to public attention about a half-century ago, the "Riffling Hitch"—which he dubbed the "Portland Hitch," after Portland Creek in Newfoundland—has helped fly fishermen hook tens of thousands of salmon on both sides of the Atlantic, and I'll wager plenty of steelhead trout as well. It was a Newfoundlander, Arthur Perry, who first showed the technique to Lee, and it so enthralled the legendary fly fisherman that in later years he went so far as to rate some rivers according to whether or not their salmon would "take the hitch." Understandable. For to have a salmon come to a hitched fly is certainly among the most exciting shows in all of sport.

Imagine my surprise, then, to discover that a significant percentage of salmon anglers I meet have never even heard of the hitch, much less know how to rig or fish it, and that only a very few recognize its full potential. The most common misconception is that the hitch works only on windless days when the water is low and warm. This is wrong on both counts...but more about that later.

For now, a quick look at the hitch itself.

Like so many nifty angling tricks, it is an offspring of that mother of invention, necessity. Back in the days of gut-eyed hooks, salmon flies (not to mention the money to buy them) were in short supply in the "outports" of Newfoundland. At Daniel's Harbor at the mouth of Portland Creek on the island's west coast, local anglers therefore sought to extend the life of their flies by half hitching their leader tippets behind their flies' heads. This took strain off the gut eyes, and much to the anglers' delight (and surprise at first, I'll bet), actually made the flies more effective on the water than when fished routinely.

And so by the time Wulff arrived, while steel-eyed hooks were already in use on Newfoundland rivers, fishing the hitch was already so deeply entrenched on Portland Creek that it had become a convention. Indeed, most Portland Creek anglers were convinced you could take salmon there on wets in no other way. Many still believe so today.

Sometimes they were able to buy them, though they were expensive for simple people living a hard life. But more often than not, old gut-eyed flies, such as this antique featherwing, were cast-offs left behind by anglers visiting Portland Creek, Newfoundland, usually British military officers whom the locals guided. The flies were treasured, and to preserve their delicate gut eyes, the half-hitches which became the essential of the Riffling, or Portland, Hitch were thrown behind the head by the thrifty Newfoundlanders. Imagine what glee ensued when "necessity being the mother of invention" proved not only be true, but that the invention born of necessity in this instance turned out to be more effective than the same flies as fished conventionally by the affluent visitors.

Hitching causes a wet fly, single or double, to plane up headfirst, then to swim across the surface trailing a V induced by the tension of line and leader on the fly's elevated head. The angler, then, can allow the fly simply to swim around at the whim of a stream's flow and currents. Or by adjusting the pitch of the rod, maybe, or employing multiple upstream or downstream line mends, or by drawing the fly over the surface by means of stripping, you can also speed your fly up or slow it down at will.

Normally, you fish the fly downstream-and-across in the conventional wet fly manner, but you can also fish it straight across-stream-and-down, three-quarters upstream, or even directly upstream. It's important, however, to adjust your swing and/or retrieve speed to prevent your fly from sinking or sputtering, as opposed to gliding smoothly. Hitched flies usually sink either because they're moving too slowly or there's excessive slack in your line or leader; they sputter, or throw white spray that puts salmon off, because they're skimming too fast, especially across turbulent water, or the angle of pitch between fly and surface is too steep—or both.

How to configure the connection knot and half hitch, or half hitches, on a fly for riffling can drive even veteran anglers batty—unless you come up with some way to spike the correct procedure to your brain.

For affixing fly to tippet, some anglers stick with old favorites such as single or double turle knots. But what's really needed is a small, minimum-profile knot, one that's reliable yet allows plenty of latitude for situating your half hitches later. So, I use a simple two-turn clinch knot reinforced by a single or double overhand knot at the end of the tippet tag to form a "jam" that prevents potentially disastrous knot slippage (see pages 13-14). This tiny knot, then, permits me to hitch a fly on either side or under the hook shank immediately behind the eye, or behind the fly's head, which although the traditional placement, can be tough on delicate dressings.

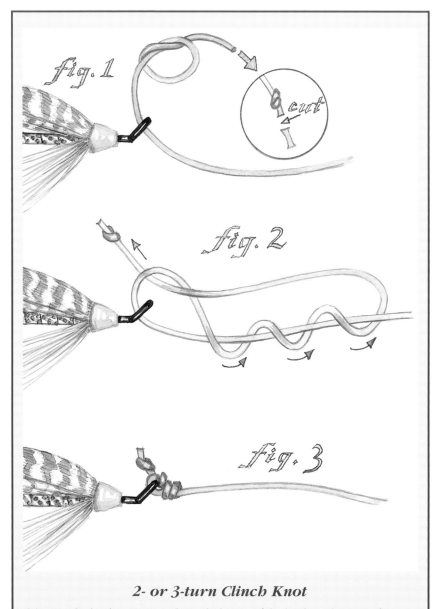

fig. 1

cut

fig. 2

fig. 3

2- or 3-turn Clinch Knot

(1) *Pass the leader tippet up through the eye of the hook as shown in figure 1.*
Then tie a simple overhand knot near the end of the tippet, as shown. Cut
the excess material close to the tightened overhand knot, as indicated
within the circle in figure 1.

cont'd

(2) With the fly hanging free, pass the standing length of tippet—that with the tightened overhand knot on the end—around the tippet itself two or three times as indicated in figure 2. Then pass the tippet tag upward through the loop you have left directly in front of the hook eye, as shown in figure 2 and indicated by the arrow pointing upwards and to the left.

(3) When the tippet tag is through the loop, clasp it between the thumb and forefinger of your left hand (assuming your are righthanded) and clasp the standing length of tippet just behind the unfinished knot.

(4) Now lubricate the knot with saliva and tighten it by pulling gently but firmly on the standing length of tippet while continuing to hold the tippet tab between your left thumb and forefinger.

(5) The snugged-up knot should appear as in figure 3, ready for the next process which is applying your hitch or hitches.

Now for the tricky part. Given that you want to half hitch your fly on one side of the head or the other, as opposed to directly underneath it (the implications of which I'll get to later), how do you remember which side the hitch or hitches should go on when the stream is flowing from left to right or right to left? Doing it the correct way is *important*. If you position your hitches on the wrong side of the head, your fly may appear to be riffling perfectly, but many salmon that take simply won't "get" the hook.

The way I remember where to position my hitches (my humble means of spiking the procedure to what's left of my brain), is *always* to hold my fly facing head-first upstream—to the right if the current is flowing from right to left, to the left if the current is flowing from left to right—and then to place my hitch or hitches on the side of the head facing the stream bank behind me. Normally, but not necessarily if I happen to be making a lot of river criss-crossings in the course of fishing a stretch of water, this is the bank from which I waded into the water in the first place. In other words, forget which is the left or which

Managing swing speed is critical when fishing the hitch three-quarters downstream. Here Galen Mercer must contend with a complex of currents to plane his meandering fly correctly. The rising salmon, visible as a swirl below Galen and slightly to his right, looked at a half-dozen presentations before finally taking just off the grass point almost directly below the angler. Galen saved the fish, but it was touch-and-go for awhile, for as all experienced salmon fishers know, a directly-downstream taker is usually difficult to land.

Hitch Presentation

With the fly aimed headfirst upstream, place hitch or hitches on the side of the fly facing the bank behind you. From position 1, your hitched fly should appear as in figure 1, and from position 2 as in figure 2. It's a cinch.

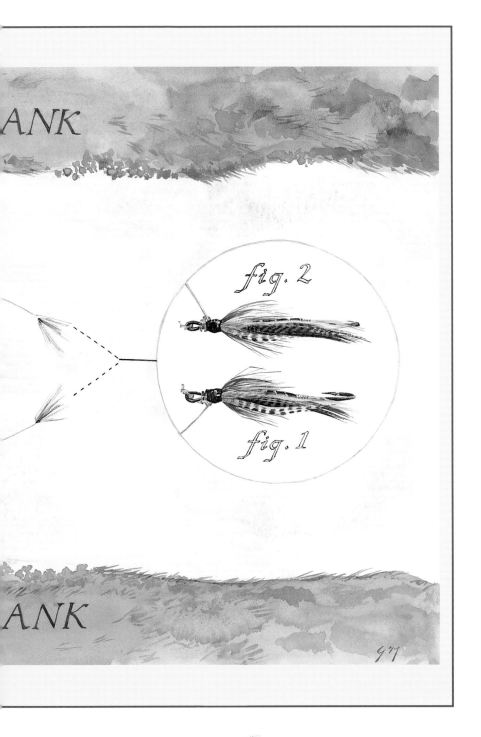

is the right bank, or which is the left or which is the right side of your fly. Too complicated. Instead, just fix in your noggin the direction of stream flow, face your fly upstream, half hitch accordingly, and you can't go wrong.

As to hitching a fly *under* the eye, or directly underneath the fly and behind the head—which, granted, eliminates having to fret about hitch placement at all—I'm really of two minds. Some knowledgeable anglers swear by this configuration, and it's hard to argue with their success. But there is a difference in the consequent behavior of the fly and thus in what salmon see as that fly passes over them.

Situating a hitch under a fly, behind either the eye or the head, causes the fly to plane across the water more or less perpendicular to the surface. This means that, notwithstanding the high-ride and trailing V, the "look" at the fly a salmon gets is much the same as when a hitchless wet fly is presented conventionally. Hitching a fly to one side or the other of the head, by contrast, cants the entire fly so the salmon then sees not only the high-ride and trailing V, but also much more of the side, or the fly's dressing, than it does when the fly is hitched underneath. How many extra salmon this enhanced visibility of fly design, color, and silhouette account for each season, I can't say for certain. But I can say that I've taken enough fish on side-hitched flies—fish I couldn't move to flies hitched underneath—to make me feel that side-hitching is more often than not worth the extra bother.

On the other hand, I usually hitch double-hook flies—except perhaps those in very small sizes (sizes 10-14)—underneath the head. For whatever reason, salmon seem to prefer the even-keeled, conventional "look" of the double-hook fly to the side-on perspective of a double-hook fly that's canted. Moreover, when you hitch a double on the side, one hook normally slices the surface all the way through the swing, which tends to prompt that off-putting spray I referred to earlier. I also find that all too often salmon seem to "get" only one hook of a side-

Configurations

The usual configurations of the riffling hitch are, from top to bottom: to the side and behind the hook eye; from the bottom behind the hook eye, which is the best way to hitch double hooks except in the smallest sizes; and from the side behind the head. When choosing the third configuration, however, be wary of damage you can do to delicate dressings, such as this featherwing Crosfield.

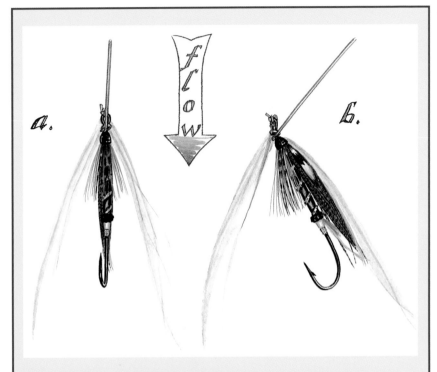

What Salmon See

When a hitch is placed under the fly, say, behind the hook eye, as in a., this is what a salmon looking up is likely to see of the fly itself, a slim silhouette not unlike what it would see were the fly being fished conventionally. The special attraction, then, is mainly the trailing V. When the fly is hitched at the side as in b., the underwater fish sees not only the V, but a full silhouette of the pattern being fished, as with this Thunder and Lightning. Over the years, I have found option b. infinitely more productive.

hitched double, allowing the free hook to act as a lever, which, because it continually pivots during the struggle, inevitably enlarging the entrance hole around the hook you're left with, enables any number of fish to escape in time.

Hitching the fly underneath, whether a double or single, is, however, the way I usually go when fishing from both sides of a boat, as in making drops down the middle of a broad pool on, say, the Restigouche or Matapédia Rivers in eastern Canada. Otherwise, when using a single hook fly, I'd be correctly hitched to fish only to the right but not to the left, or vice versa. Never forget that just because a fly appears to be riffling well doesn't mean it is—at least as far as successful hookups are concerned.

Alternatively, of course, you could always side-hitch your fly, then fish it only to, say, the right of the boat first, reel in all your line, reconfigure your hitch or hitches, then fish to the left. I rarely do this because: (1) it's a helluva lot of bother, (2) it tends to throw off my fishing rhythm and hence diminishes the pleasure of the overall angling experience, and (3) it seems, for some inexplicable reason, to drive most guides crazy, no small concern when you consider it is the guide you must depend upon for well-positioned drops, among a host of other jobs that can make or break a day.

If you do decide to side-hitch your flies while out in a boat in the middle of a river, though, all you need remember is to face one bank, hold your fly so its head is pointing upstream, then half hitch the fly on the side facing the bank *behind* you. Or put another way, if the current is flowing from left to right and you want to fish to the right side of the boat first, you turn sideways, aim the fly headfirst upstream (that is, to the right), then hitch it on the side of the head facing toward you.

Now let's take a look at precisely how half hitches ought to be made. Betcha some of you will really be surprised by how dramatically the subtlest variation in "throwing" this simple knot can alter how your fly swims and therefore what the salmon see.

CONFIGURATION

"**T**here's a right way and a wrong way to do everything," my iron-willed English grandfather used to tell me when I was a lad. "In fact, there's usually a wrong way to do the right thing." While Grandfather's primary focus was principle, his words apply no less to more practical matters: stacking wood, dressing flies, or creating the "Riffling Hitch" by throwing one or more half hitches over the head of an Atlantic salmon or steelhead fly.

Although the half hitch is a simple knot, the slightest variation in the way you form it, then affix it to your fly for hitching, will dramatically affect how the fly swims, how salmon see it, and perhaps even more to the point, whether they "get the hook" when they take. Doing it right demands not only that you know on which side of the fly's head to place the half hitch or hitches, but exactly how to make and configure one or more hitches so your fly will swim to best advantage.

In the first chapter I wrote, "If you position your hitches on the wrong side of the head, your fly may appear to riffle perfectly, but many salmon that take won't 'get' the hook." In point of fact, I may better have said that your fly "may appear to riffle *even better* [when hitched on the wrong side], but many salmon..." Here's why.

When you hitch a fly on the wrong side, no matter how you configure your hitches, the fly's head tends to plane up, both higher and more readily. This is because the tension on the fly is *indirect*, coming from under and across the fly's head, rather than *direct*, from the side facing the angler. Thus, it's easier "to

A tastier spot for presenting the hitch three-quarters downstream could never be found than this one on Iceland's Laxá I Adaldal. The water speed is moderate, the surface slick and fish could be lying almost anywhere, either resting or holding. The author began fishing short and has now worked out a length of line which will take hitched salmon handily, especially since, given the configuration of his hitches, no hook-setting will be necessary.

get the fly up" and keep it there throughout the swing than when the fly is configured as I have suggested. The problem, though, is that the point, barb, and bend of the hook face *toward* the angler when hitched on the wrong side, which is away from the direction a salmon is most apt to turn—the direction of its momentum—after taking a fly, hitched or rigged conventionally. Therefore, unless you set the hook sharply, or luck out, more often than not it fails to stick in the salmon's jaw. Instead, as the salmon turns in the natural course of returning to its lie, the fly simply slides or rotates out of its mouth. (See illustration on pages 28-29.)

To hitch the fly correctly as described, you aim it headfirst upstream and place your hitch or hitches on the side facing the bank behind you. Having done so, the point, barb, and bend now face outboard, or toward midstream, as shown in the illustration. When the salmon follows, takes, and extends its course as a consequence of its momentum in heading back to its lie, the hook usually lodges squarely in the bony corner of the jaw without recourse to hook setting. In other words, the salmon hooks itself.

Now, at the risk of creating chaos out of order, I should say there *are* exceptions. Suppose the salmon is lying tight to the bank from which you're fishing, directly below you, or closer to the shore than where you are standing when you present your fly. In each case, the salmon may indeed turn counter to its momentum, or toward midstream, and thus might better "get" the hook with its point, barb, and bend facing inboard. Unless you happen to *know* the fish is there, however, in which case you may deliberately configure your hitches on the "wrong" side, it's better to gamble that it's not there or opt to place your hitches *under* the hook. Given that you're three-quartering downstream, doing so saves you wasting up to 45 degrees of fly swing.

Adjustments in how you hitch a fly can often be made if you are lucky enough to have a "spotter" looking down on the salmon to see how they are behaving with each fly presentation. Otherwise, play it as suggested in the text.

Rights and Wrongs

Given the casting position of the angler at lower left, figure 1 shows the "wrong" (a) and "right" (b) ways to configure a Riffling Hitch. Note: fly (b), facing headfirst upstream, has its hitch on the side of the head facing the bank behind the angler. Figure 2 shows the attitude each fly maintains while planing across the surface throughout the fly swing. Fly (a) cants with its hook-point facing inboard, or toward the bank, while fly (b) cants so the point faces outboard, or toward midstream. That's the way you want it be-

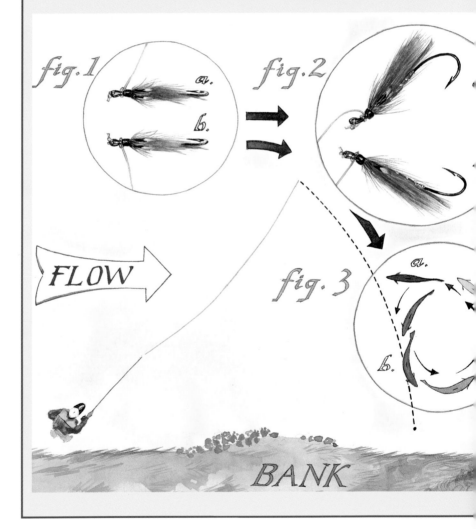

cause a salmon leaving its lie, as in figure 3, position (a), normally intends to return there, following a course something like the one indicated by the salmon and arrows in this schematic. As the salmon follows the fly, its momentum carries it across and downstream until it intercepts the fly somewhere along the dotted line that suggests the fly swing. When the fish, the red salmon (b), takes the fly, it typically does not yet know it is hooked and so continues to turn in the direction its momentum dictates.

Figures 4 and 5 show what's likely to happen if you've hitched the fly on the wrong side, which is (a) in figures 1 and 2, and the right side, (b), in the same figures. In figure 4, the fly is in the salmon's mouth, but it faces away from the corner of its jaw, which means that as the fish turns, it's likely to rotate out of the mouth. Conversely, in figure 5, the hook faces back toward the corner of the jaw, and it's therefore likely to become lodged there by the momentum of the fish and the direction in which the salmon is turning. The fish in figure 5 hooks itself.

This angler is near the right bank of a river flowing from his left to his right, but the lesson would apply no matter where he stood in the stream. Were he casting from the opposite bank with the river flowing from his right to his left, figure 1 (a) would become the correct hitch configuration because the hook would be facing, as in figure 2 (a), toward midstream, and again, a salmon following the natural course of its pursuit would most likely hook itself.

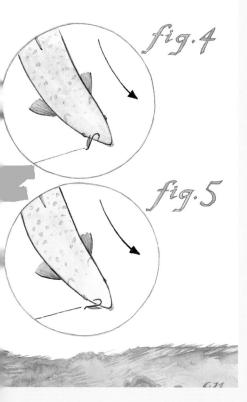

fig. 4

fig. 5

See the V trailing the fly on the slick water ideal for hitching salmon in the photo above. Hitching this water is relatively easy and often your best bet is an even swing. By contrast, hitching broken water, such as that shown in the photo opposite, is a matter of great control, as various currents play games with your fly as it planes. The so-called "meandering" drift of the fly

Another exception may be the salmon you've "teased into," as Ernest Schwiebert has aptly put it. Having been attracted, but not raised by a previous cast, the fish comes for and takes your swinging fly *before* the fly reaches the water directly over its lie. Again, however, unless you have somehow seen the salmon and how it's been reacting to your fly before its rise, or have a "spotter" stationed on the bank overlooking the pool, such takes are hard to predict. Barring one of those irresistible, though in actuality usually deductive, "hunches" that great anglers such as Schwiebert are prone (and wise) to play, my advice is to stick

is more common to the latter conditions. To achieve a meandering swing on smooth water, you must manipulate your rod and line while making certain your fly doesn't die as a consequence of guessing wrong. To get an even swing on broken water normally suggests keeping your rod tip low, your line straight and "leading" your fly across the surface.

with the odds. Hitch your fly either on the correct side, in which case you may want to set the hook and pray luck is on your side, or underneath the head.

Then there's the salmon that has risen several times, confirming its tendency to turn counter to its momentum after each rise, a relative rarity. To be on the safe side, I remain inclined—if I'm going to adjust at all—to hitch my fly under the head. But there *are* instances when a salmon has turned counter to its momentum after each of seven or eight rises when reconfiguring the hitch to the wrong side may be worth the risk. Think on this one, though, before leaping out of the blocks. I once had a salmon come eleven times without taking, turning counter to its momentum after each of these rises, only to rise a twelfth time, take, turn *in* the direction of its momentum and *not* get the hook.

Now look ahead to the tying illustrations beginning on page 34. Beyond the tying instructions, note the positions of both of my hands. Each finger has a specific job to do and I've tucked out of the way all the fingers I'm not using at a given time. As I learned long ago from legendary Catskills fly tyer Walt Dette, this is essentially the way you should fashion all knots—the clinch, turle, blood, and other knots—to attain greatest efficiency during the tying and maximum breaking strength in finished knots.

Note that a hitch or hitches may come off the fly with the tippet inclined either upwards or downwards, which can serve specific purposes depending on stream conditions. The tippet-upward configuration works best for hitching across sluggish to moderately swift water. Because the tippet-downward configuration tends to plane your fly lower in the surface film, it ensures that in faster water your fly doesn't throw off that white spray salmon don't like. By contrast, you should always configure multiple hitches alternatively—one over, one under, or vice versa, the extended middle finger—or in the form of a clove hitch, since this provides maximum security on the hook. A hitch that slips off a hook, after all, isn't a hitch at all.

I should also point out that the surest way to secure a hitch to a fly is probably the method still used by local anglers on Newfoundland's Portland Creek where the hitch originated. They form and twist their loops as the illustrations here show, but then take them all the way back around and under the bend of the hook, as in completing a turle knot, before pulling the hitch tight to one side or the other of their flies' heads. With all

Not only was Walt Dette the "fly tyer's fly tyer," he was also an "effi-ciency expert," or the guy to whom engineers bring problems they can-not solve. I learned much from him during the almost 30 years we were friends. Among them was whether angling or fly tying, "you should make every part of your body count." It is from that foundation that he taught such gems as making use of each of your fingers whenever you tie a knot, the Riffling Hitch included.

---

due respect to these executors of tradition, though, their method presents one potentially disastrous problem. If a hitch does man-age to slip off the hook—which, granted, doesn't often occur—it produces a wind knot in the tippet a few inches in front of the fly's head. And, boy, I *hate* to lose salmon to wind knots.

Here's how to "throw" a half hitch quickly and efficiently for riffling under various stream conditions.

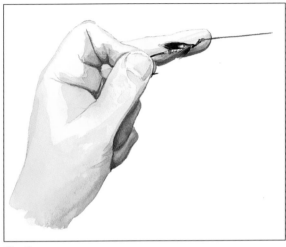

Fig. 1

Figure 1: After affixing tippet to fly, face the head of the fly upstream, and clasping the bend of the hook firmly between thumb and forefinger, extend your middle finger directly behind and parallel to the fly, while tucking away your ringfinger and pinkie. Meanwhile, clasp your tippet between your thumb and forefinger of your opposite hand just far enough back from the hook eye to make it convenient to work. The other fingers on this hand, too, should be tucked into a fist and stay that way throughout the knot-tying.

Figures 2 (a) and (b): To finish the half hitch with your tippet inclined *upward*, begin to form it by making a loop around your extended middle finger, drawing the tippet material first *under* that finger, as in Figure 2 (a). To finish with the tippet inclined *downward*, begin the half hitch by drawing the material *over* the middle finger to start the loop, as in Figure 2 (b). (Since all subsequent steps are identical, we've chosen to show only the sequence that begins with the under-the-finger loop.)

Figure 3: Complete the loop by drawing the tippet material under, around, and under the extended middle finger, as indi-

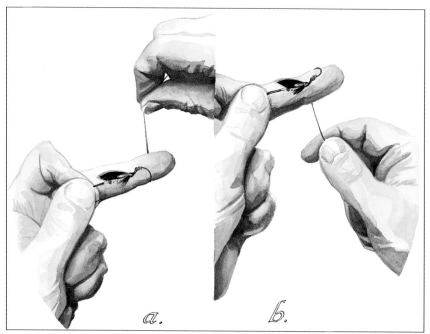

Fig. 2

cated by the arrow. To expedite this step, you want to extend the middle finger behind the fly slightly while pinching the bend of the hook somewhat tighter. Tightening the pinch causes the head of the fly to rotate inboard, that is toward you a bit, and back toward the palm of your hand just a little, which keeps the fly out of your way while you complete the loop.

Fig. 3

Figure 4: Clasp the base of the loop you've created where the monofilament intersects. You accomplish this by rotating your middle finger toward you a bit, at the same time relaxing the tension on the loop ever-so-slightly.

Fig. 4

Figure 5 (a) and (b): Slide the loop off your middle finger, as shown in Figure 5 (a). To do this, swivel your middle finger slightly away from you while relaxing the pinch-grip on the bend of the hook. This returns the head of the fly to roughly the same position as when you began. Now begin to rotate the loop as when you began. Next, begin to rotate the loop, as the arrow in Figure 5 (a)

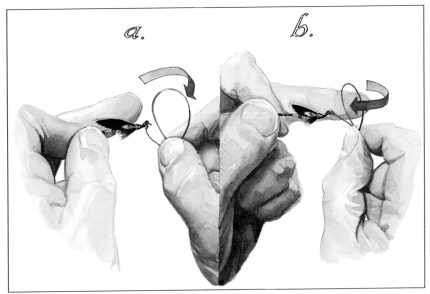

Fig. 5

suggests so the material that came off the back of your middle finger revolves toward you. Then, re-extending your middle finger as much as possible, for it will help guide the loop during this maneuver, continue to rotate the loop toward you, as indicated by the arrow in Figure 5 (b), until the loop's opening is directly in line with, and just in front of, the head of the fly.

Figure 6: Using the middle finger of the hand holding the fly and the thumb and forefinger of the hand holding the base of the loop, guide the loop over the hook-eye. Then, press your extended middle finger to trap the far side of the loop securely at the point directly opposite where you want the tippet to emerge.

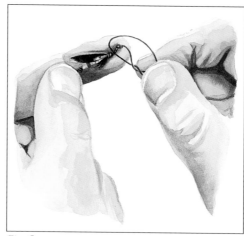

Fig. 6

Figure 7: Now carefully slide your right thumb and forefinger from the base of the loop until they are clasping only the tippet material snugly. Then, draw the half hitch tight by pulling gently but firmly on the tippet.

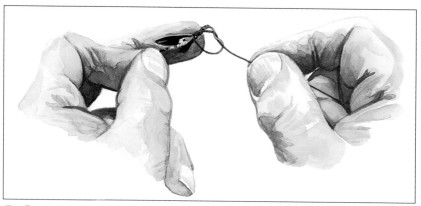

Fig. 7

Figure 8 (a) and (b): Note that on hitched fly (a), the tippet is inclined upward, and thus the fly will plane high as it swims across the surface. This is a result of having begun your half hitch with a loop drawn under and around your middle finger, as in Figure 2 (a). On hitched fly (b), by contrast, the tippet inclines downward to make the fly swim lower. This happens when you begin with a loop drawn over and around your middle finger, as in Figure 2 (b). Remember: when you throw multiple hitches on a fly, which large and heavy flies may require, always alternate loops, one over and one under the middle finger, for maximum security. Remember, too, it's the second hitch you throw that determines the incline of your tippet.

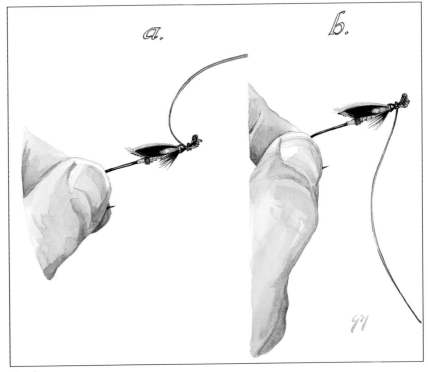

Fig. 8

Next, why not enter what I'll bet is unchartered water for most salmon fishers and steelheaders, even those who fish the hitch regularly.

WHENS, WHYS — AND WOWS

E ven by the standards of Iceland's coldest, windiest, rainiest summer in memory, the day was *awful.* The sky lay almost on the river and an icy gale tracked a mix of lashing rain and occasional sleet as much parallel to the earth as toward it. The hood of my rainjacket crackled in my ears and the tips of my fingers stung as my brother George and I, bent over like potato-diggers, trudged side by side from a warm car to the west bank of Iceland's Laxá I Adaldal at Oddahylur. That's Point Pool, or to most North Americans who fish "Big Laxá's" Árnes beats, just "Upper-4."

"The juice worth the squeeze, ya'think?" George hollered into the wind.

"Oh, you're gonna take a fish here, for sure." I'd have bet my last dollar on it. "But you ain't gonna believe how."

By Laxá standards, Upper-4 is a short piece of water, no more than eight or ten steps downstream on black lava sand once you've worked out a full length of line. It doesn't look like much, but it *always* holds salmon. So, I use it to experiment—to change flies two or three times, try new techniques. And despite the dreadful conditions, I was about to walk George through one of those experiments, although he wouldn't know it until it was all over.

Setting my rod down against a hummock, I waded out a few yards with him, then asked to see the fly he'd been fishing. "Cut it off," I told him, rummaging through one of my boxes, "and try this." I handed him a size-8, double-hook Green Butt.

An excellent southpaw caster, George fished out the Green Butt, followed by a little Night Hawk, a Blue Charm, and a Stardust, all in a quarter-hour or so. "Now here's what I want you to do," I said, somewhat smugly I'm afraid, as I handed him a size-10, double-hook Red Butt. "Just to keep 'em honest, fish this through quickly." Which he did with the same results the other flies had wrought—not a fin.

"What now?" he asked.

"Now you catch a salmon," I told him. Even through misty glasses, there was no mistaking his doubtful expression. *This is really gonna be worth freezin' your ass off for,* I thought, grinning in my mind. I was *that certain.*

"Hitch the fly. Go ahead, hitch it and fish it out."

George looked down at the little Red Butt and then at me.

"You gotta be shittin' me," he said, his doubtful look

Here I am on Upper-4 with one of those salmon that just can't resist the hitch, come rain or come shine. This lovely 16-pounder is being netted by longtime Icelandic guide and friend Steini Stefansson.

fast-forwarding to one suggesting his "big brother" and lifelong pal had finally lost his mibs. "The hitch on a day like this?"

"You wanna catch a salmon or not?" I said, allowing my grin to show.

A Portland Creek veteran, George can throw a hitch around a fly as nimbly as anyone. Even with his cold-stiffened fingers, he had his Red Butt ready for the wash in seconds.

The salmon came about where I thought it would, just ahead of where Laxá bulges over a protruding plate of lava. No hesitation—or as 18th century author John Cleland wrote so quaintly in *Fanny Hill,* "Nothing loath." It wasn't a big salmon, but it was a *sure* salmon, and within minutes it was writhing in the net.

"Wouldn't'a believed it if I didn't see it," George crowed, shaking his head. "You sonofabitch." He was laughing that wonderful, infectious laugh his brother and countless friends know and love so well.

"Don't you go talkin' about our mamma like that," I said, slapping him on the back. "That fish on that fly—*hitched*—was a sure thing. It happens every time here on days like this."

Trouble is, many anglers wrongly think of the Riffling Hitch as a proposition strictly for warm days, calm weather, moderate to low water, a relatively slick surface, and above all, a small fly. Yet, I can't think of a single medley of weather and water conditions that hasn't yielded me at least one salmon to the hitch somewhere—and doubtless would have yielded more had I sufficient confidence to always practice what I preach.

I don't pretend to understand all the "whys," but the following is a small sample of what I've learned over the years. (Anyone sitting on any, or all, the answers, by the way, please let me hear from you.)

First, let's take aim at this bit of traditional "wisdom:" *When the air temperature is colder than the water temperature, your best bet is a sinking-tip line.* Fine, but only up to a point. It's true

It may not look so, but this was the single coldest day I can ever remember fishing salmon. There just weren't enough clothes or gloves to stay warm. Yet, three Grimsá salmon that refused everything fished conventionally took a hitched Night Hawk.

that when the air is colder than the water, salmon typically ignore flies swimming conventionally at shallow depths—flies they
can't take without breaking the surface with their bodies—and
that this dictates a strategic change to lines that "take flies
down." But I have found no such reticence among salmon reacting to the hitch. *Au contraire.* They seem to relish bolting off
the bottom and exposing their heads, backs, and tails to the
open air while capturing hitched flies—even when the air is
much colder than the water and high winds (the wind chill fac-
tor) increase the contrast all the more dramatically.

Since many anglers think the hitch works best only on calm
days, the whole issue of wind has proven very interesting. Ever notice how landlocked salmon go nuts for streamers trolled through—
not beneath—the whitecaps on wind-swept lakes? Well, anadromous salmon often seem no less flushed at the prospect of snatch-
ing flies that create wakes as they skitter over and through the chop
on stream surfaces—or at precisely those moments when so many
anglers feel compelled to switch to immediate lines to *minimize*
the influence of chop on their conventional fly swings.

You should know, though, that controlling the swings of
hitched flies on windy days demands considerable "touch," that
is, a thorough understanding of how to position your rod and
line at all times to counter Aeolian mischief. Remember, pace is
critical, and it's your job to set it. Otherwise, you're surrendering
not only to the whim of external force, but to that of dumb luck.

More often than not—given, say, upstream and downstream
winds—keep as much line *on the water* as possible, or put another way, keep your rod tip low. This prevents wind from
pushing, pulling, or bowing your line, and thus swamping or
hoisting your hitched fly, or making it race willy-nilly across the
surface. But as always, there are exceptions. A headwind, for example, or one three-quartering upstream toward you, may dictate that you "lead" your fly by raising your rod tip while rotating it inboard ahead of the swing.

A very stiff upstream wind seems an unlikely time to fish the hitch, but it can work sometimes under such conditions when all else fails. Note how Galen Mercer controls the speed of his hitching fly by mending his line upstream, or with the wind, to slow the fly down ever so slightly as it planes across the surface. Mastering such subtleties are the signs of a truly skillful angler.

Nor is pelting rain grounds for eschewing the hitch, as many anglers suppose. Amid all the oval spatterings of calm rainy days or the scudding "pitchforks" of windy ones, you may not be able to spot the V-shaped wake that a hitched, skimming fly creates, but in rain it proves a veritable lightning rod to salmon, especially fresh fish that otherwise might not leave their lies until the storm has abated. Watch, too, for the magical moments right after downpours when the air clears and warms, and the wind, if any, dies. For as Joe Cullman, chairman emeritus of The Atlantic

Salmon Federation, might say, they're really "Miller Time" for the hitch.

Or what about those deep, turbulent waters studded with boulders that anglers and guides alike often shrug off as fishless. Not fishless at all, the hitch has taught me. The only way I've ever found to "pull 'em up," however, from such spots is to fix it so hitched flies pop in and out of the white-water sloshes and plane smartly across the "tongues" and "mirrors" characteristic of such stretches. Here, too, you must learn to ply your fly through the course of the swing, making sure it's "up" at the critical instants when trailing salmon are most apt to take. And because the takes are likely to be violent, given the water's swiftness, it's

Few anglers use the riffling hitch in rough weather, but here artist, fly tyer extraordinaire, and brilliant salmon fisher Galen Mercer plays a salmon hooked on the hitch during a driving rainstorm.

also prudent to hold a loop of, say, six or eight inches of fly line between your reel and rod grip to absorb some of the shock.

The hitch is also useful *strategically*, both to 'spot' salmon and to bring reticent risers to steel. A quick hitch over that lie where "you just know there's a fish" after having failed to stir any action by the usual means, often gets results. A hitch can also work as "something out of left field"—to show to salmon that have looked at patterns fished conventionally but have stubbornly refused to latch hold. Or as a teaser to re-interest fish that have risen several times to your offerings, then seemingly called it quits. Or as a trick to tweak the salmon you really hope to hook on the *next* presentation, that is, by showing it a "super-attractor" such as one of Joe Hubert's Sheep series (see next page). The possibilities, in short, are virtually endless.

But the most amazing revelation has been the Riffling Hitch's effectiveness during times of bitterly cold and sometimes turbid water, perhaps very early in the season, when traditional wisdom insists the only way to take salmon is to go straight to the bottom with high-density sinking lines and brass tubes, or some unwieldy equivalent. While it's true that most salmon might ignore conventionally fished flies, regardless of size, virtually anywhere in the water column except right in their faces, they *will*—for some reason I can't begin to explain—come all the way to the surface to take hitched flies. In other words, the same salmon that wouldn't rise to, for example, a size 1/0, double-hook Green Highlander swinging one inch to one foot below the surface, will often come up, chase, and grab a hitched size 2, 4, or even 6, single-hook fly of the same pattern.

Caveat: While fly fishermen underuse the hitch on many, even most, Atlantic salmon fisheries, some rivers are "over-hitched." Their salmon actually see too few flies fished conventionally. Remember, just as "wormed" or "spooned" rivers can be duck soup for the fly rodder who suddenly appears on the

Galen Mercer and I came up with this variation of Joe Hubert's Sheep series fly, great "comeback" flies when salmon won't return to conventional dressings, hitched or not. Although we call it the Sundown Sheep, it seems to work at any time of day or weather. Here are the makings.

Tag:	Oval silver tinsel, just a couple of turns
Body:	Black floss
Rib:	None
Wing:	4 parts black bucktail over 1 part light-to-medium blue bucktail, 3-4 times hook length, into which is mixed a moderate amount of multi-colored (Rainbow Mobile) Flashabou
Throat:	Shiny midnight blue cock's hackle, doubled, wound several turns and pulled down
Head:	Black

scene, a conventionally fished fly is often the answer on waters where anglers have hitched salmon to death. Simply put, the Riffling Hitch is a tool, another wrinkle, and not the philosopher's stone.

Now we're going to look at the most unusual—and under-rated—way of all to fish the hitch.

"ABOUT FACE"

I f you picture an angler fishing the hitch, what do you see? Most likely the river breaking around the backs of his knees, his hamstrings, or his fanny. What you're not likely to visualize is water swirling in front of his knees, against his quadriceps, or if he's in deep enough, sloshing at his belly button. Why? Because the hitch has always been reckoned by most as a downstream-only technique. In fact, I don't think I've observed more than a half-dozen salmon anglers fishing the hitch upstream in all my years astream. A potentially costly mis-conception. For given the right circumstances, including by the way, dour or stale fish that have seen more than their fill of flies, wet or dry, fished conventionally, little more than an "about-face" can result in the steel of the hook ending up where you really want it.

Well, now that I've gotcha, I have to confess that quite a bit more than an "about-face" is really involved. Actually, upstream hitching is sort of tricky, requiring that you be able to reliably estimate the *vis viva* of moving water, as well manipulate flies so you never lose control. In other words, you have to be able to gauge precisely, for instance, the speed of flow, probable ramifi-cations of intervening surface currents on fly behavior, then know exactly *how* to keep hitched flies "up" and on course.

You'll soon learn, too, upstream hitching is impossible on some waters, such as powerful rapids or stretches so swift you just can't stay apace of their velocity in order to keep your flies "up," no matter how small and light their hooks or how fast you draw or strip line. Fortunately, though, such waters also tend to coincide with where salmon are least prone to tire of seeing

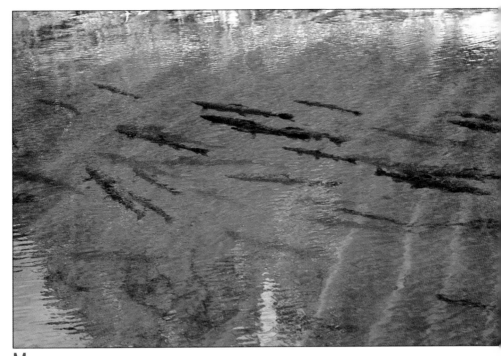

Mobbed-up salmon like these, even when "stale," are often quite literally duck soup when you fish an upstream hitch. Often, having never seen the technique before, two, three, even four fish will chase the fly at the same time. The hardest part is keeping your cool.

conventionally-fished flies, or more apropos to this study, hitched flies three-quartered downstream.

Ultimately, the key, of course, is to keep your fly's head up so the fly skims over the surface without dipping and diving on the one hand, or throwing that demon spray on the other. Usually you'll find this easier if you position yourself for three-quartering upstream, as opposed to presenting directly upstream. Three-quartering better enables you to utilize rod pitch and line mends, coupled with drawing and stripping, to maintain constant tension on your line and so your hitched fly. Also remember that normally downstream mends speed flies up, upstream mends slow them down. But when it comes to upstream hitching, there *is* a rub.

Two examples of prime upstream hitching water and resulting explosive takes. This stretch, from Québec's small Malbaie River, is slow, even languid; the other,

Say your fly is lagging. Your understandable inclination will be to mend downstream to increase your fly's speed, as when you three-quarter downstream. But when you retrieve a hitched fly three-quartered upstream, the effect will be different and hence the results different, too. To your surprise, you'll notice that a downstream mend causes a bow to form in your working line *ahead* of your fly which, if not removed quickly, will cause your fly either to swing outboard which may be okay if you are just prospecting, or first to droop then sink like a stone, a disaster.

However, by throwing an upstream mend—the last thing you'd consider when fishing downstream—though it may stall your fly for an instant, it will in practice serve, by tossing your working line further away from, that is, above your fly, to paradoxically increase the short-term tension on the fly. This tension,

from the Ste. Anne also in Québec, is relatively swift, but not too swift to be able to keep "ahead" of the fly's downstream progress with a snappy retrieve.

then, will prompt the fly to ride higher—not lower—which is your ultimate goal. In either event, though, waste no time in stepping up your rate of drawing or stripping line, as well as perhaps even raising your rod tip, if only temporarily. In other words, do anything to restore the essential tension on everything between your rod tip and your fly.

Generally speaking, you'll also want to ignore salmon fishing's old taboo against false-casting. Our sacred downstream pick-it-up-then-lay-it-down presentation technique that uses the water to load the rod simply won't work when presenting hitched wets upstream, any more than it will when fishing dries. Reason? Except in rare circumstances, such as turbid or extremely high water, salmon simply won't tolerate wet flies whistling over their heads, then plopping down in front of them. So be prepared to

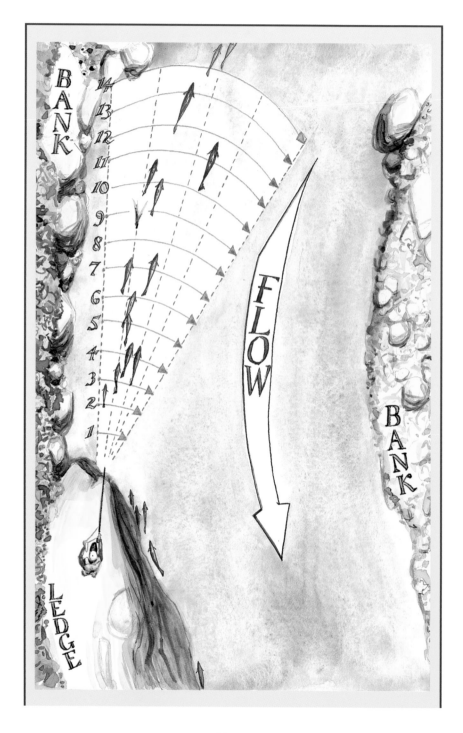

Presentation Strategy

A system of water and lie coverage is essential to effective upstream hitch-ing, just as it is to all wet fly salmon fishing. Note that for purposes of illus-tration, the author has moved to the ledge side of the river. Whether or not he can see the fish before him is really irrelevant. He begins with a short line (1) working the water from the bank side outboard in wedges until he reaches a position as indicated by the end of each arc and arrow where he feels his effective coverage has ended. He then proceeds by extending line the length of his arm to work upstream, next to position and arc 2, then 3, and so forth, until he recognizes that at position and arc 14, he has reached the limit of his effective water coverage. With each cast, remember, he must strip line and keep that excess line under control at all times in case he hooks a salmon. Given where he has opted to present from, he must also work out in advance how and where he will play a fish, even if it means crossing the river somewhere to get to the lower bank, in this case a beach, to land his quarry.

make at least a couple of false-casts ahead of each upstream hitch presentation. But bear in mind, too, that covering a lot of water remains critical; so to maximize line speed, you'll want to use the "fastest" line available. Then to minimize line-shadow passing over target lies, you should also use the longest leader you can handle. Twenty feet *isn't* too long for upstream hitching and even longer can be better if you can manage it.

Another must is to evolve a water-coverage plan that often proves more intricate than the typical one for hitching down-stream. This is because one section of a pool, say, will accom-modate upstream hitch presentations and required retrieves, while another will not. You may encounter a nice current-edge, for instance, adjacent to a side eddy, either, or both, holding salmon, where hitching upstream will be a snap, though just outside that current edge, the flow speed will dictate that the water be covered in a conventional downstream direction, hitch or no hitch. So, plot in advance, making sure your physical pres-ence going one way doesn't blow the potential for eventually going the other. It should go without saying that you can't blunder through salmon while wading downstream, for instance, then presume they'll somehow fancy your fly minutes later just because you approach from below.

Since every stretch of salmon water is different, I can't be more explicit. I can say, however, that not to "worry" potential takers should be a high priority. And so, since the slacker water most compatible with upstream hitching tends to be located near shore, not in mid-stream, it's often best to approach fish or likely lies from downstream first. Even at that, though, be certain not to venture too far out or you'll muck things up no less than were you to make an impolitic approach from above. Sloppy wading costs fish. Step on their heads, step on their tails. *Pas différence.*

When upstream hitching, I like to cover a wedge of water, sort of like a wedge of pie, beginning close to the bank, beach or shore, then progressing outboard with each successive presentation. Be methodical. Never extend line, for instance, until you've covered every likely lie within range of the length already out. Then, just as when fishing downstream, extend by the length of your arm. Less line compromises efficiency, more risks water coverage gaps.

Which brings us to two critical points regarding upstream hitching not usually germane to fishing downstream: (1) what to do with the excess working line you accumulate with each retrieve of your fly, and (2) promulgating a reliable strategy for raising salmon that "look" but don't take your first presentation.

Point 1: There are two options. First, and best, is to make loops of retrieved line in your left hand (assuming you cast right-handed) as you draw and/or strip. Your second option is to simply allow excess line to trail or gather in the water. If you follow the second course, check your line often to be sure it isn't snagged or snarled. Even a tiny knot can catch in a rod guide. So, try to place trailing line in the same place during each retrieve—off your left hip, for instance. Also don't fail to consider

When fishing upstream or down with a wet fly, hitched or not, for optimum water coverage extend line the length of your arm between casts.

that since water causes friction, greater energy is required to drag trailing line off the water, which translates, in turn, to the need for greater power to cast the same distance were that drag not present, as when you hold loops. A logical extension of this drawback is the need for more false-casts per presentation, which takes more time, meaning that in the course of an outing your fly spends less time in the water than it otherwise would and should.

Although it takes practice, every angler, I believe, ought to know how to make and hold loops. It's easy, really, if you bear in mind just a couple of fundamentals. The longer the strip, for instance, the fewer strips it takes to accumulate enough for a working loop. Moreover, loops should be collected so the *last* you clasp is the *first* to leave your hand when shooting line into your next cast. So, as you take the line needed to keep your fly up and moving, first you collect enough line to make a sizable loop, then roll it over and lay it on your palm. Beware that one loop never lies atop another. Rather, the first you gather should cross the middle of your palm, with each successive one placed slightly outboard of the last, that is, toward your fingertips. At first you may have to check from time to time to be sure the progression is correct, but in time with constant repetition, the routine becomes second nature.

Point 2 is *really critical*. It's obvious that if a fish rises, but doesn't take, you're not likely to bring the fish back unless it sees your fly again. This means paying constant attention not only to the direction of each cast you make and the heading your fly is on when a fish shows, but *exactly* how much line was out when the fish came. The only practical way to accomplish this is to measure and count every draw or strip of line during each retrieve. My system is to always draw or strip line from the point at which it emerges from under my forefinger on the rod grip to a spot just off my left hip, or a spot just off my left side if wading deep. Either way, the spot should never vary even an inch. Meanwhile, I count *every* draw and/or strip so I'll know exactly how many I've made should I have to repeat the cast. Failure to follow such a procedure will leave you either totally lost when a fish comes but refuses your fly, or dependent on Lady Luck, whose attention I, for one, crave only in Vegas.

Although some will disagree, including Galen Mercer, my own fishing partner, I like my rod tip angled as low to the water as I can practically position it when I fish the hitch upstream. Why? (1) I get a direct and unobstructed view of everything that's happening in front of me; (2) I can raise my rod if need be to take slack out of the line on the water and by so doing, help keep my fly "up"; (3) line-bow between rod tip and surface is minimal, so stripping is truer, more direct and without the hesitation that sometimes causes hitched flies to sink, and (4) being pri-

When retrieving line, as noted in the text, every angler should learn to make loops to be held in his or her non-casting hand. Many anglers never do so, however, because they fear snarling during the following cast. To avoid this very real concern, learn to take loops onto the palm of your hand so that each loop lies next to the other and in such a way that the last loop made will always be the first loop to leave your hand when you shoot line during the next cast. Then, if there is an occasional snarl—as there inevitably will be—disentangle it as quickly as possible, for if a fish takes your fly, the clash of the bulky snarl against the stripping guide of your rod as the fish takes line is bound, at best, to break the fish off, at worst to break the fish off and damage your rod.

marily a salmon fisherman, thus positioned, I can either slow my fly or even "lean into" a potential taker if necessary. Bear in mind that Atlantic salmon, unlike most gamefish species, including steelhead, tend to be discouraged when flies appear to be getting away in the final seconds before they intend to take. So, often you must, in effect, "feed" a salmon your fly or risk having it give up just prior to the moment of truth.

A reversal of the usual, meaning that all good anglers do what is most applicable to the situation. In the first photo, Galen Mercer, usually an advocate of the high rod for hitching, hitches the Matapedia in Québec with his rod low. In the second photo, old

When salmon take the upstream hitch, more often than not they tend to follow flies some distance before latching hold. For some reason, too, their takes are apt to be even more explosive than those to hitched flies fished downstream. What is more, given that the upstream hitch usually lends itself better to slower-moving water than its downstream equivalent, you'll frequently find it quite difficult to decide on which side of your fly's head to throw your hitch or hitches. From pool to pool and stretch to stretch it often varies, depending on the overall character of the water, as well as from where in the wedge of pie referred to above a salmon happens to come. Therefore, the "safest" place to rig your hitch(es) is often underneath, rather than

"low rod" Art goes for a high rod technique on a Laxá I Adaldal pool in Iceland. The nature and speed of the water, speed and complexity of currents, among a host of other variables, dictate your technique of the moment.

to either side of, the head, *unless* you know where the salmon is lying and can be reasonably certain which way it will turn as it returns to its lie, given predictable momentum. If you have a good handle on all this, by all means rig your hitch(es) on whichever side of the head you determine optimal. Having said this, though, and bearing in mind that salmon may not turn at all for awhile after they take, but instead continue swimming *toward* you, always be prepared to set the hook just as you would if you were fishing dry flies.

Next, we'll take a look at some hitching fly patterns that have "traveled" well for me over the years from river to river and country to country.

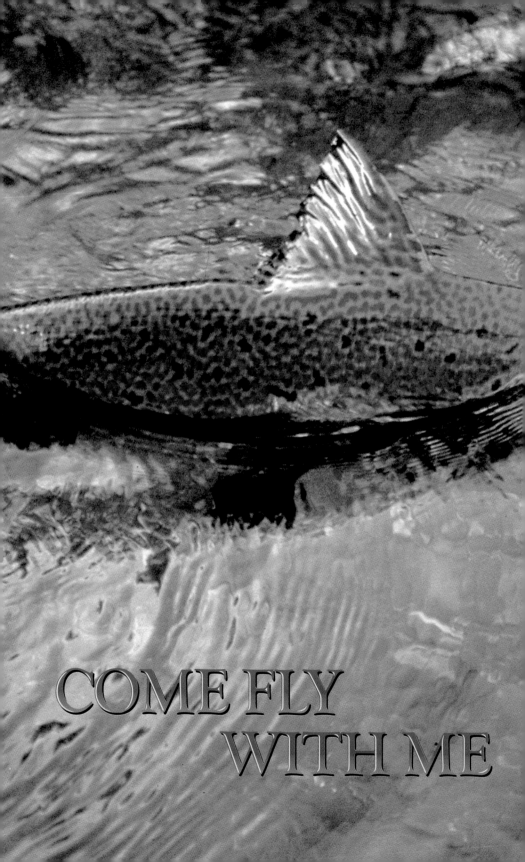

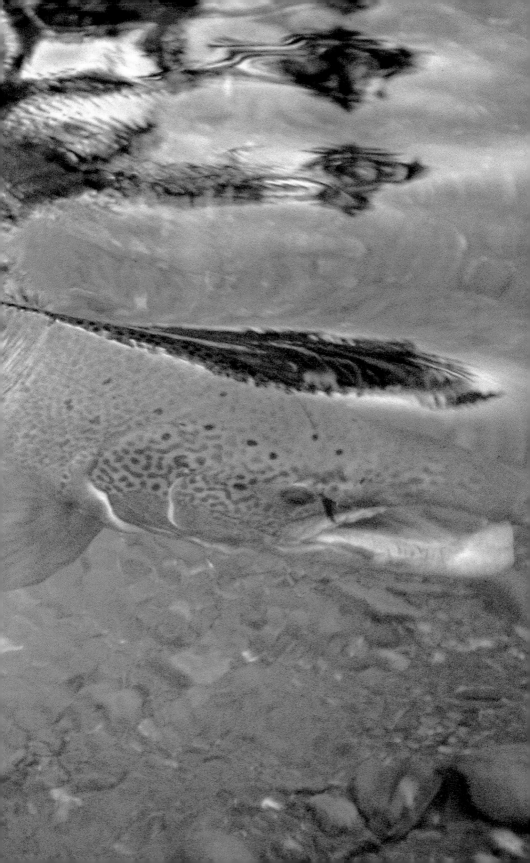

"The fly that works best is the fly that's fished most," or so goes an old saying with which I'm not inclined to agree—especially with flies rigged for the Riffling Hitch. Since my first hitch-hooked salmon back in 1967 on Newfoundland's Portland Creek where hitching began, I've caught hundreds with my fly so rigged. I now have a strong sense that pattern, size, and silhouette all play integral roles in the effectiveness of this remarkable technique. Moreover, how you dress a fly—that is, the materials you use and where and how you affix them to the hook—are of paramount importance.

This chapter is a distillation of what I've learned about hitching fly patterns that work best *on the rivers I fish*. I know that at least some will travel well to other fisheries on both sides of the Atlantic. But take none of this as gospel. There are hundreds of salmon rivers I've never seen, much less fished, and so the best teacher in the end no doubt will be your own experience. I will say, however, that I'm convinced that there's no salmon river in the world, including the biggest, brawniest, and coldest, where the hitch won't work at one time or another—more often than not when all else fails.

One constant of an effectively hitched fly is that it planes across the surface, leaving in its wake a well-defined, but not sputtering, V. As long as the fly planes properly and you, not the river, are in absolute control of its demeanor, the fly's route through its swing—whether a predictable sweep or an erratic meander—isn't of the utmost importance. Certain salmon, you'll soon learn, clearly favor a predictable swing, while others, perhaps out of aggression or playfulness, seem to get excited by a more irregular turn.

What salmon usually *don't* like are flies that hitch fitfully, that are "up" one instant, "down" the next, planing flawlessly at times, spitting showering spray at others. But then the behavior of a fly often begins with the choice of pattern and how the fly tyer turns it out of his or her vise.

But why are salmon attracted to the hitch in the first place? I believe the attraction is much like that of a marlin to a bait trolled off the stern of a sportfishing boat. The disturbance of the boat catches the marlin's attention, then the bait, skittering on its side as if wounded or otherwise helpless, triggers the fish's instinct to strike. Similarly, a salmon investigates the V behind a planing fly, then spots the fly itself, especially if the fly is canted to one side, and then the salmon responds to the same instinct as the marlin, just as it would snatch a vulnerable tidbit of food at sea.

I normally eschew fly fishing "rules"—too many exceptions—but with respect to flies for hitching, you might want to keep the following in mind: (1) given conditions, use the smallest fly possible, at least one or two sizes smaller than the flies you'd fish conventionally; (2) lighter-weight hooks, including low-water singles and doubles, and even wets tied on dry fly hooks, are generally preferable to heavy, standard irons; (3) slim, sparsely dressed flies usually outperform bulkier dressings as they're easier to keep "up"; and (4) try to have your flies tied somewhat forward on the hooks, not necessarily as far forward as traditional low water dressings, but far enough to minimize the risk of fast-moving salmon pinching the feathers or picking the hook points.

Marlin

*I've always been capti-
vated by the similarity
of behavior of my two
favorite gamefish, the
Atlantic salmon and the
blue marlin, where it
regards their fascina-
tion with skittering or
planing prey. The in-
stinct, I think, is much
the same, especially
since salmon, in rivers
for long periods and
long since given up as
"non-takers," are sud-
denly turned on by a
hitched fly. The dy-
namic is much the
same with the marlin,
which sees both the V-
shaped wake of the
sportfishing boat and is
attracted to it, then is
drawn to the Vs trailing
behind the baits, teasers
or feathers, skimming
along in the boat's
wake. The marlin, like
the salmon, homes on a
V, then viciously attacks
the bait, just as the
salmon does the fly. A
wonder and wonderful.*

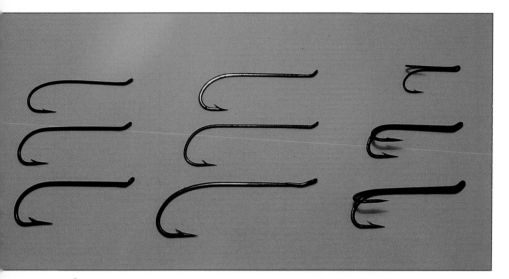

As for every other dimension of salmon fishing, some hooks are better suited to dressing hitching flies than others. Here are the choices of Galen Mercer and myself (in columns from left). *First Column:* Orvis Salmon/Steelhead Dry Fly Hook (1644-00) size-8 single shown; Partridge 'Wilson' Dry Fly Hook (Code 01), size-4 single shown; Herter's Low Water Single (difficult to find), size-4 single shown; *Second Column:* Partridge Single Low Water Hook (Code N), size-6 single shown; Hardy Single Low Water Hook, no longer available (hunt them up if you can and treasure them), size-6 single shown; Sprite 'Gaelic Supreme' Low Water Salmon, size-1 single shown; *Third Column:* Turrall Low Water Double Hook, size-8 shown; Partridge Double Low Water (Code Q), size 6 double shown, and Partridge Double 'Wilson', (Code 02), size-16 double shown.

To expand on these thoughts.

1. Salmon *will* react to, say, a 1/0 or 2/0 hitched fly, but that same fish is just as likely to take a hitched fly of the same pattern in sizes 2, 4, or 6, even if the water is high and cold. Why I'm not sure, but I suspect the answer involves the palpability of the V. I do know, though, that once the fish has risen to a hitched fly, the odds of the fish "getting" the hook increase dramatically as the hook size decreases.

2. Since you should try the hitch under what many view as unlikely conditions, such as high, cold water, your hooks must be of the finest quality, not flimsy affairs prone to turning into spears when you slug it out with heavy salmon. Test the temper of all hooks before buying them and insist your tyer does the same before he or she dresses flies for you. Remember: if you can readily bend a hook, so can a struggling salmon or steelhead.

3. While I favor a slim fly silhouette, I do like a full, dense throat on my hitching flies. Choose stiff, sheeny cock hackle, double it, then wind it on the hook. Avoid the expedience of "false hackles." Full, stiff hackles help keep a hitched fly's head cocked upwards through the swing, while sheen, by enhancing the radiance of the fly, may account for the somewhat enigmatic appeal to salmon of smaller hitched flies.

4. Salmon often take hitched flies both violently and unexpectedly and thus are singularly unforgiving of those little timing errors we all make (but are inclined to dismiss) when fishing conventionally. For instance, deprived of the luxury of reaction time to "feed" a fly to a fish, your using a fly tied forward on the hook enables you to regain your edge by ensuring the salmon's jaw meets steel before it does feathers or fur.

By the way, although a double-hook devotee, I prefer singles with sharp points and short barbs for hitching.

Ideally, you should tie salmon flies specifically for hitching. *Leave lots of space between the head of the fly and the eye of the hook, so there's room for one or more multiple hitches.* To have hitches repeatedly "pop off" in the course of fishing is a drag, not to mention what a pain it is to have to pick off or clip through half hitches that you've crammed between a fly's head and eye.

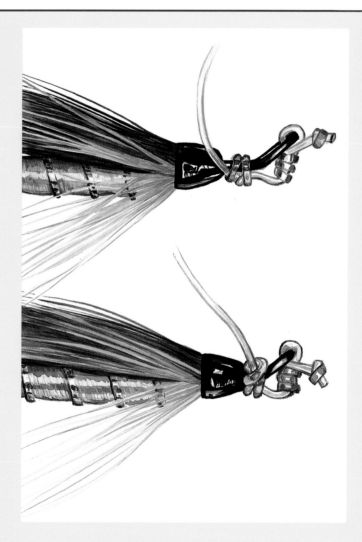

Right and Wrong

For best results with the Riffling Hitch, tyers should fashion flies specifically for use with the technique. The head of the upper Laxá Blue is situated well behind the hook eye, leaving plenty of room to throw one or more half-hitches. The head of the lower Laxá Blue is so close to the hook eye there's insufficient space for multiple hitches, for they pile up on one another. Yet the lower fly is perfectly well dressed to accommodate a knot, such as the turle, for fishing conventionally.

The effectiveness of hitching flies often depends on little things—nuances, if you will. A stiff wing of moose mane, for instance, is a particular favorite of Portland Creek regulars. What also helps is a dash of striking color, such as a fluorescent red or green butt underpainted (on the hook) with white lacquer so the floss never loses its brilliance. Moreover, bearing in mind the function of the flies, single-wrapped, rather than double-wrapped, tinsel bodies save weight. Learn to jettison components that experience suggests are extraneous to attracting salmon. My favorite hitching fly, for example, which I'll get to later, has no rib at all.

I favor relatively simple flies at the extremes, that is, bright or dark in overall appearance, rather than in between. I prefer the Colburn Special, for instance, a green but decidedly luminous fly over, say, the Green Highlander, one of my all-time favorites for fishing conventionally. I also incline to a Fox Fly or Green Butt for hitching, rather than the Black Dose, the fly on which I've probably taken more salmon while fishing conventionally than on any other pattern. There are some mid-range exceptions, however, notably the Night Hawk (reduced), the Hairy Mary, and the old reliable Logie.

Other patterns I like for hitching include: in the bright category, the Silver Blue, Crosfield (yellow head), Laxá Blue and Cullman's Choice, named by its creator, Lee Wulff, for Joseph Cullman III, chairman-emeritus of The Atlantic Salmon Federation; and among dark flies, the Blue Charm (featherwing), Blue Butterfly, Stardust, and Red Butt. Remember, though, certain flies may very well outperform my choices on your favorite river. So don't hesitate to work your hunches and, if you would, drop me a line when you come up with a river- or country-specific winner.

While the "bright-day-bright-fly and dark-day-dark-fly" axiom applies to a significant degree to the Riffling Hitch, if I had to choose only one fly for hitching, regardless of conditions, it would be an almost shamefully simple pattern I call the William Williams Blue Charm that I named for a charming old fly tyer, long gone now, who lived in Pittsfield, Massachusetts. What there is about this least

William Williams Blue Charm

My favorite hitching fly is the William Williams Blue Charm. It's so simple, and yet so effective. I only wish I entirely understood its magic myself.

elaborate of patterns that makes it so effective, I haven't a clue. But believe me, it charms salmon like no other fly I've ever discovered.

Here are the makings *(see illustration above): Tag:* Fine oval silver tinsel. *Tail:* Golden pheasant crest. *Body:* Black silk floss, scraped with a scissors or knife blade to fray the silk slightly. *Rib:* None. *Throat:* Sheeny midnight blue cock hackle. *Wing:* Bronze mallard, the darker the better. *Topping:* Golden pheasant crest. *Head:* Black.

Some of the hitching patterns I prefer, like the Silver Blue and Green Butt, are so popular among fly tyers worldwide there's no need to repeat their recipes or illustrate them here. Others, however, are regional favorites or adaptations of standards and not so widely known. The Stardust is mine alone. Illustrator-fishing partner Galen Mercer and I spun off the Blue Butterfly from an already effective pattern, the Ingalls' Butterfly, which Maurice Ingalls of Fort Lauderdale, Florida, had originated.

Blue Butterfly

Tag:	Four or five turns of fine oval silver tinsel
Tail:	Medium blue hackle fibers, half the length of the hook shank
Body:	Twisted strands of peacock herl and blue mylar tinsel
Rib:	None
Wing:	Blue calf's tail (kip) of a rich, medium blue, tied in "butterfly" style
Throat:	Medium blue cock hackle, tied as a collar, with two turns behind the wing, the remainder in front
Head:	Black

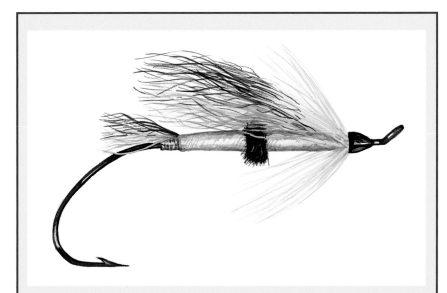

Colburn Special

Tag: Fine oval silver tinsel

Tail: A small bunch of apple green calf's tail (kip), one quarter the length of the hook shank under an equal-sized bunch of black calf's tail (kip) of the same length

Body: Fluorescent apple green floss in a torpedo ci-cigar-shaped taper, with a joint of black ostrich herl in the middle

Wing: A small bunch of apple green calf's tail (kip), over which is a similar bunch of black calf's tail (kip)

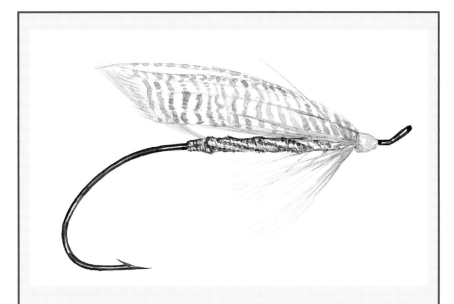

Crosfield

Tag:	Fine oval silver tinsel
Tail:	Golden pheasant crest
Body:	Embossed flat silver tinsel
Rib:	None
Throat:	Silver Doctor blue cock hackle
Wing:	Gray mallard sections, back to back
Head:	Yellow

Cullman's Choice

Tag:	Fine oval silver tinsel
Tail:	None
Body:	Fluorescent apple green floss
Rib:	Oval silver tinsel, one size larger than that used for the tag
Throat:	Sheeny white cock's hackle
Wing:	Glossy black hair, such as squirrel tail
Topping:	Golden pheasant crest
Head:	Black

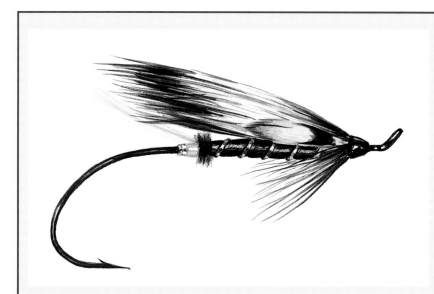

Fox

Tag:	Fine oval silver tinsel
Tip:	Fluorescent yellow-orange floss (lacquered)
Tail:	Golden pheasant crest
Butt:	Black ostrich herl
Rib:	Oval silver tinsel, one size larger than that used for the tag
Throat:	Black cock's hackle
Wing:	Gray fox guard hairs
Sides:	Jungle cock
Head:	Black

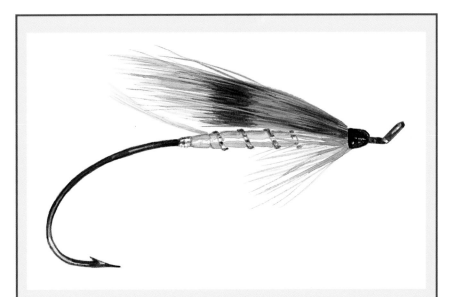

Laxá Blue

Tag:	Fine oval silver tinsel
Tip:	Fluorescent yellow-orange floss (lacquered)
Tail:	Golden pheasant crest
Body:	Pale blue floss
Rib:	Oval silver tinsel, one size larger than that used for the tag
Throat:	Silver Doctor blue cock's hackle
Wing:	Gray squirrel tail dyed a rich Silver Doctor blue
Head:	Black

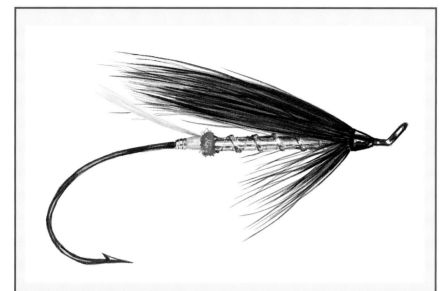

Night Hawk (Reduced)

Tag:	Fine oval silver tinsel
Tip:	Golden yellow floss
Tail:	Golden pheasant crest
Butt:	Bright red wool, spun into a "rope"
Body:	Flat silver tinsel
Rib:	Oval silver tinsel, one size larger than that used for the tag
Throat:	Black cock's hackle
Wing:	Glossy black hair, such as squirrel tail
Head:	Black (narrow ring of red lacquer optional)

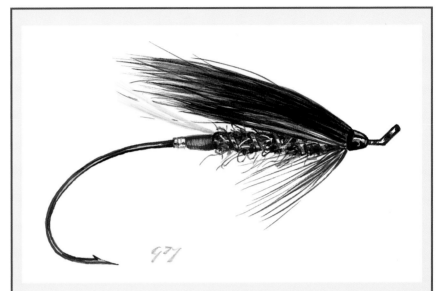

Stardust

Tag: Fine oval silver tinsel

Tip: Midnight blue silk floss, tied approximately 1-½ times a normal tip's length

Tail: Golden pheasant crest

Body: Black "Sparkle Yarn" dubbed loosely on dark blue silk, then picked out when dubbing is completed

Rib: Oval silver tinsel, one size larger than that used for the tag

Throat: Sheeny midnight blue cock hackle

Wing: Glossy black hair, such as squirrel tail

Head: Black

To wrap it up, I just can't resist a few yarns about the most interesting salmon I've risen, hooked—and in some cases, anyway, even managed to wrestle from rivers—while fishing the hitch.

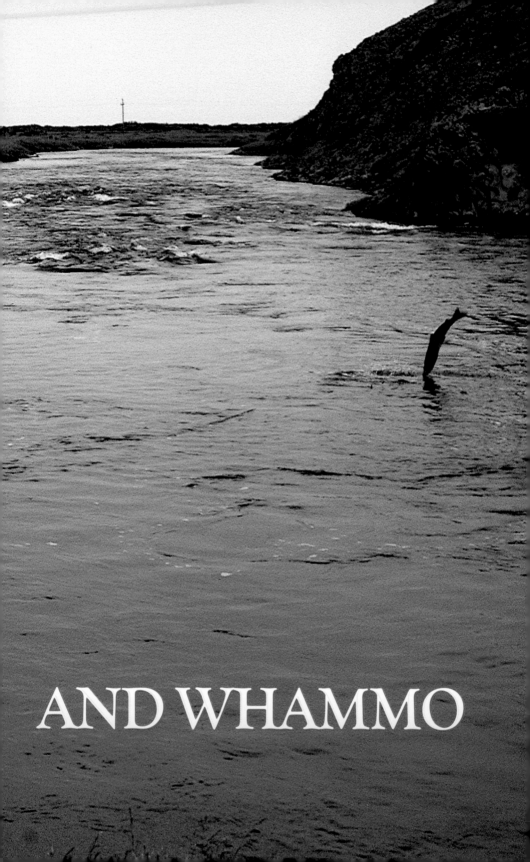

AND WHAMMO

I f there's anything more memorable than catching big fish, it's catching interesting fish—fish that come out of especially tricky places, for instance, or taunt anglers week after week until somehow, by hook or crook, you supply the right symmetry of tackle and technique to get the job done. Indeed, actually landing a fish sometimes isn't as important as having had the "right stuff" to bring it to steel, as brief as the liaison may turn out to be. Among the most remarkable experiences I've had in my decades astream involved lost fish, including salmon that I consider myself lucky just to have hooked.

Not surprising, I suppose, that many of these *beatae memoriae* involve fishing the Riffling Hitch. The hitch, after all, is something of a surprise itself, one of those inexplicable, happy accidents that serve to sweeten our sport and that we'll understand fully only if we come back as salmon (or steelhead). Until then, all we can do is rejoice in it by using it for all it's worth.

I'll never forget being shown how to tie the hitch back in the 1960s on the rocky beach at the Runout Pool on Portland Creek, Newfoundland. My guide was the late Riley House, a man of great wit and extraordinary insight into salmon behavior. Nor will I forget the hours of backhand casting necessary to compensate for the seemingly omnipresent upstream wind that just "kills'ya" when you fish the right-hand side of that pool, nor the changing of flies, as often as not more to rest a weary casting arm than out of any real need for a new pattern, nor trying to get the "feel" of raising and lowering my rod tip as I sought to master maintaining control of my planing flies as they crossed the currents.

Nor how, suddenly, while I was still working the upper third of the Runout, a salmon materialized below and outboard of my fly and followed and followed, forever it seemed, until finally in a burst of speed and a glorious swirl, it snatched the fly and we were off to the races.

This first hitched salmon was an acrobatic 12-pounder—not a bad fish for Portland Creek in those days—but what I recall most vividly aren't its jumps or long runs across the broad pool, my screaming reel, or even seeing the salmon finally secure in the netbag. What I recall most vividly is how *radiantly blue* that salmon's back appeared as it trailed my Riffling Hitch before the hookup.

Then there was that cold, bright, windy day in the early 1970s when my fishing partner, the late Dave Danzig of Schenectady, New York, toppled into Iceland's Laxá I Adaldal and I was left to my own devices while he returned to the lodge for a change of duds. I'd explored a likely slice of Lower Beat-5 with a small Crosfield fished conventionally, but I suddenly thought, "Why not the hitch?"

Oh, but didn't the old adrenaline flow even as I snipped off the Crosfield and threw the hitches in front of the head of a lovely Silver Blue given me that very morning by Ernie Schwiebert. And the exquisite anticipation with each of the mere dozen casts it took before a bright grilse bolted the fly, then greyhounded all over Laxá's emerald surface. My first unassisted Laxá salmon lives in my memory for its own sake, of course, but how I caught that fish...now that was, and remains, *the thing*.

Why? To be a successful Atlantic salmon angler, just as to succeed at any sport, involves a major psychological component. To

Splendid Isolation

Where it all began for Lee Wulff, for me, and for so many others—a mistake gone right, the miracle of the Riffling Hitch. Newfoundland is a beautiful island with about 200 salmon rivers, including some of the best in North America. I know of none on which the hitch doesn't work. This Galen Mercer painting, in my opinion, personifies the beauty of country, the feeling of joy in the splendid isolation where you are not only watched over by your Newfoundland guide, no doubt a hitching specialist himself, but by the ghosts of so many Newfoundland hitchers-past.

produce strategically, or guilefully, if you will, boosts your self-confidence. You become more inclined to extend yourself, to reach, and perhaps most important, to improvise.

I remember another day, on another Icelandic river—Laxá I Kjos on the southwest coast—a day to which I usually refer only to illustrate the importance of getting your fly down to the salmon when air temperatures are colder than water temperatures. It was a nifty enough experiment, really, and a valid one, producing three fish from a small pool with a sinking-tip line, none with a floater. But what I've never revealed before is that, despite the frigid air and warm water (by Icelandic standards) that afternoon, I also took a brace of salmon on the Riffling Hitch from my "laboratory" pool.

Moreover, I suppose if I'm "to dare to call my soul my own"—though even in seeking this, note I corrupt the context of a line from Elizabeth Barrett Browning—I should also come clean to anybody who may still recall how, during one rugged mid-1970s summer on the Matapédia, I managed 23 of 29 salmon logged from the river's public water during a two-week period. The fact that 19 of them fell to the hitch has been my secret until this moment. (Had Lee Wulff been fishing instead of yours truly, I have no doubt he'd have tallied 28, a fortnight's limit in those days.)

But I've also hitched up my share of salmon that demand no confessions. For instance, during an "off day" on Russia's Ponoi—yes, even Utopia occasionally has them—when I declined to follow the prevailing wisdom in favor of the hitch and quickly sparked the salmon back to life, giving me a banner outing. Or a 22-pounder tucked into the curl at the head of Cullen Rock Pool on the Matapédia that I brought up with an upstream hitch-and-retrieve after any number of anglers had vainly tried to take her by conventional methods. Or all the salmon I've hitched up over the years from the sluggish "flats"—long written off as "worming water"—on Iceland's diminutive Ellidaár. And

Evidence. Two of those salmon taken on the hitch during that Matapedia week long ago when the technique remained my secret and other anglers went fishless. If I had to do it over again, well, I don't know. I do know I would have kept the waistline, if wishes could be horses. Today, I do know I would also have released the fish.

having unlocked the secret to riffling up the otherwise stubborn salmon of Point Pool on Laxá I Adaldal's Árnes beats under the most likely conditions, later shared with my brother George and described in detail earlier in this little book.

Two other Laxá salmon also come quickly to mind—one I knew was present, but disinclined to rise, the other a "surprise" born entirely of faith in the water and the power of the hitch—

both fish taken from small "potholes" belonging to a farmstead called Knútsstaðir, or to most North Americans, Árnes' Upper Beat-6.

The stretch above, behind, and below the farmhouse is slick of surface and somewhat difficult to read, but a real joy to fish once you get a feel for it and come to trust that salmon are always there, though often reluctant to take. One pothole is near Laxá's west bank, perhaps 200 yards upstream of the farmhouse, and I fish it religiously each time I draw the beat (sometimes at the expense of time on pools where taking salmon is a surer thing). But during this trip, try as I might, I hadn't seen, much less risen, a salmon there all week.

Hitched Salmon

I can see it as if it were yesterday. My first hitched salmon, caught at Portland Creek, Newfoundland, and its "radiantly blue" back as it followed my planing fly.

Just as I was walking dejectedly to the car with my back to the river, I heard that most onomatopoeic of all salmon fishing sounds, the telltale "cush" of the "maybe taker," a salmon that hasn't quite rolled but hasn't quite jumped either. The sound had come from the pothole's principal lie, and I immediately went back to the water to begin covering the spot with a series of flies. It wasn't until I'd tried at least a half dozen in various sizes, all fished conventionally, that I tried the hitch, and then it took only one presentation of a hitched number-6 William Williams Blue Charm to hook an elegant 14-pounder.

Why Not the Hitch?

While fishing the "pothole" on Iceland's Laxá I Adaladal conventionally with several flies, I thought, "Why not the hitch?" How sweet it is.

The second fish from a Knútsstaðir pothole was in water just below the farmhouse. Here, Laxá glides over black sand and a series of lava shelves sunk deep enough and worn smooth enough by centuries of flow not to disturb the surface much. There's one spot off the west bank I particularly like, although it's never been particularly generous to me.

This season was no exception. I'd given the pothole a whack each time I was on the beat but had so far drawn a blank. But that particular evening was perfect, the kind you dream about when fishing on Laxá—not a breath of breeze, the sky purple as darkness approached, the surface oily.

So I bore down on the spot, fishing five flies, all doubles, all conventionally—a Green Butt and a Stardust, both in size 6, a Fox and a Night Hawk, both size 8, and a number-2 Thunder and Lightning. *Nada.* Then I rigged the same William Williams Blue Charm with the hitch, and—*whammo*—a lovely 16-pound hen took. She put up a magnificent battle and ended up safely boxed in one of the river's in-stream caches, to be held for hatchery stock. Thus, I had not only the joy of knowing I'd taken a fine salmon strategically, but was left with the hope that she'd provide Laxá with offspring that would take my flies in future seasons.

During the last four decades, I've caught more Atlantic salmon from the world's great rivers than any quintessentially Irish-American, middle-class kid born in Yonkers, New York, could ever have imagined in his wildest dreams. I've had more than my share of double-digit days and enough blank ones to instill in me a firm conviction that at least a reasonable mastery of strategy and technique is crucial to maximum success astream, as well as to the fullest enjoyment of the sport.

I've learned that catching a salmon becomes more than simply catching a salmon—*if* you can heighten the experience with the taste of personal victory. Learning to rig and fish the

Ultimately, this is what it's all about, the song of the salmon fishing experience—the angler bowing to a leaping salmon, and the guide, such as he is, at the ready. To borrow at bit from two of my favorites, salmon conservationist Orri Vigfusson of Iceland, and Frank Sinatra, the chairman of the board, "It's hitchcraft..."

Riffling Hitch is a means to that desirable end. Lee Wulff, unquestionably the greatest salmon angler North America has ever produced, understood this absolutely. This is no doubt why he held the technique—learned from Newfoundlander Arthur Perry in what was then a very remote area—in such high regard and sought so tirelessly to promote it as epitomizing the best in sport and sportsmanship. Believe me, Lee was right on the money.

Index

About the Author

Art Lee takes pride in being a fishing writer who really fishes. The work from his pen flows from his line as he fishes more than 200 days each year at home and abroad, where he has caught about every species of sport fish from bluegill to blue marlin. He has fished the most storied fresh and salt waters in the United States and Canada, South America, Europe, the Caribbean, Africa, and the Pacific.

Art is a three-time winner of the Orvis Writing Awards for excellence in the fields of outdoor and conservation journalism. In his career, he has written hundreds of articles for a wide range of publications, including *National Geographic, Sports Illustrated, Field & Stream, Outdoor Life, Fly Rod & Reel, Wild Steelhead & Salmon, Sports Afield, Fishing World Magazine,* and *Gray's Sporting Journal.* He has published more words than any other writer for *Fly Fisherman* Magazine, which he has served since its earliest days, first as Northeast Field Editor, then as Contributing Editor, and now as Editor-at-Large. He is also the first-ever Editor-at-Large of *The Atlantic Salmon Journal,* the official publication of The Atlantic Salmon Federation, as well as the west coast–based *Wild Steelhead & Salmon* Magazine.

Lee and his wife Kris live and work in the Catskill Mountains of New York.